SIMON P. EL

GRAECO-ROMAN EGYPT

SHIRE EGYPTOLOGY

Cover illustration:
Mummy portrait of a bearded man (detail).
Hibeh; third century AD.
(Fitzwilliam Museum, Cambridge.)

British Library Cataloguing in Publication Data:
Ellis, Simon P.
Graeco-Roman Egypt.
— (Shire Egyptology Series; No. 17).
I. Title.
II. Series.
932.
ISBN 0-7478-0158-4.

To Bulge.

Published by
SHIRE PUBLICATIONS LTD,
Cromwell House, Church Street, Princes Risborough,
Buckinghamshire HP27 9AJ, UK.

Series Editor: Barbara Adams.

ISBN 0 7478 0158 4

First published 1992.

Printed in Great Britain by
C. I. Thomas & Sons (Haverfordwest) Ltd,
Press Buildings, Merlins Bridge, Haverfordwest, Dyfed SA61 1XF.

Contents

Acknowledgements

I would like to thank John Ruffle, Roberta Tomber, Steve Sidebotham and Mylene Francescon, for expert advice during the writing of this book. Pete Woolford read through the text, helping me to avoid several mistakes. In addition I thank Jacqueline Fearn of Shire and Barbara Adams for making it possible. The dynastic chronology is based on that of Dr William J. Murnane and acknowledgement is made to him and to Penguin Books for its use here. Finally I must thank all those individuals and institutions who allowed me to use their illustrations in this book.

List of illustrations

Chronology

Predynastic Period	*c.*5000-3300 BC	
Protodynastic Period	*c.*3300-3050 BC	
Early Dynastic Period	3050-2613 BC	Dynasties I-III
Old Kingdom	2613-2181 BC	Dynasties IV-VI
First Intermediate Period	2181-2040 BC	Dynasties VII-XI(1)
Middle Kingdom	2040-1782 BC	Dynasties XI(2)-XII
Second Intermediate Period	1782-1570 BC	Dynasties XIII-XVII
New Kingdom	1570-1070 BC	Dynasties XVIII-XX
Third Intermediate Period	1070-713 BC	Dynasties XXI-XXIV
Late Period	713-332 BC	Dynasties XXV-XXXI

GRAECO-ROMAN PERIOD

Macedonian Kings	332-305 BC	*Ptolemy I governor after death of Alexander the Great 323 BC.*
Ptolemaic Period	305-30 BC	

305-283	*Ptolemy I Soter*
285-246	*Ptolemy II Philadelphos*
246-222	*Ptolemy III Euergetes*
222-204	*Ptolemy IV Philopator*
204-181	*Ptolemy V Epiphanes*
181-145	*Ptolemy VI Philometer*
145	*Ptolemy VII Eupator*
145-116	*Ptolemy VIII Euergetes II Physcon*
116-107	*Ptolemy IX Soter II Lathyros*
107-88	*Ptolemy X Alexandros*
88-80	*Restoration of Ptolemy IX*
80	*Ptolemy XI Alexandros II*
80-58	*Ptolemy XII Neos Dionysos Auletes*

		58-55	*Berenike*
		55-51	*Restoration of Ptolemy XII*
		51-47	*Ptolemy XIII*
		51-30	*Cleopatra VII Thea Philopator*
		47-44	*Ptolemy XIV*
		44-30	*Ptolemy XV Caesarion*
Roman Period	30 BC - AD 395		
		30 BC-AD 14	*Augustus*
		14-68	Julio-Claudian Dynasty
		69-96	Flavian Dynasty
		96-98	*Nerva*
		98-117	*Trajan*
		117-138	*Hadrian*
		138-192	Antonine Dynasty
		192-235	Severan Dynasty
		235-284	Over thirty minor rulers
		284-324	Diocletian and the Tetrarchs
		306-363	Constantinian Dynasty
		364-392	Valentinian Dynasty
		379-450	Theodosian Dynasty
Byzantine Period	AD 450 - 642		
		450-457	*Marcian*
		457-474	*Leo I*
		474-491	*Zeno*
		491-518	*Anastasius I*
		518-578	Justinianic Dynasty
		578-582	*Tiberius Constantine*
		582-602	*Maurice*
		602-610	*Phocas*
		610-641	*Heraclius*
		641-668	*Constans II*

1
Introduction

For the majority of people Egypt is the land of the Pharaohs, the pyramids, the Sphinx and hieroglyphic inscriptions. If people do know of Egypt after the Pharaonic period then they think of it as a time of decline. The only well known Egyptian from this later period is Cleopatra. Early archaeologists shared this view. They were primarily interested in the Pharaonic sites and when they came across remains of the Greek and Roman period they cleared them out of the way with very little recording and hardly a mention in their publications.

At the end of the nineteenth century this perspective was changed through the discovery of masses of ancient papyri (figure 1). Papyrus is the reed grown in the Nile valley that, when pressed, formed the traditional writing material of ancient Egypt. Comparatively few papyri have been found dating from the Pharaonic period, but many thousands have been found from the Greek and Roman periods. Moreover the vast majority were written in a form of everyday Greek, which is more widely known amongst scholars than ancient Egyptian. Nowadays there are few major museums in Europe without a collection. Unfortunately, since most of them look like scraps of writing paper, they are not the kind of objects that are regularly exhibited. In this book particular papyri are given a conventional reference to the collection in which they are found: for example PLond stands for papyri that are now in the British Museum in London, and PTebt stands for papyri that were originally found on the site of Tebtunis. A full list of the abbreviations is given in chapter 8.

The papyri were so enticing because scholars hoped to find lost literary masterpieces by the major Greek and Roman authors. Some were found, but most were in fragmentary condition and, while they have improved our knowledge of classical authors, few new major works have been discovered. Because of this approach researchers were more concerned with the papyri themselves than with the places where they have been found. We thus have considerable information about the everyday life of Egyptians during the classical period, but less archaeological information on topics such as architecture or pottery.

The principal excavators from Britain during the late nineteenth and early twentieth centuries were B. P. Grenfell and A. S. Hunt. They worked at a number of sites, but the most important was Oxyrhynchus, from which some fifty volumes of papyri have now been published (POxy). Hunt also worked with C. Edgar to produce the most important English translation of papyri, publishing four volumes in the Loeb Classical Library.

The papyri collected by Hunt and his collaborators, like those found by other scholars, consist of virtually every kind of document imaginable. There are letters, laws, census returns and contracts for work (figure 1), property or other services. Shorter documents are simple lists, accounts, receipts (figure 2) and other miscellaneous notes. The excavators may not have discovered many literary texts, but the documents form an infinitely wealthy resource for understanding the everyday life of ancient times. Normally archaeologists and ancient historians have to rely on literary texts that were written by the intellectuals and aristocrats of a civilisation, but in the case of Graeco-Roman Egypt

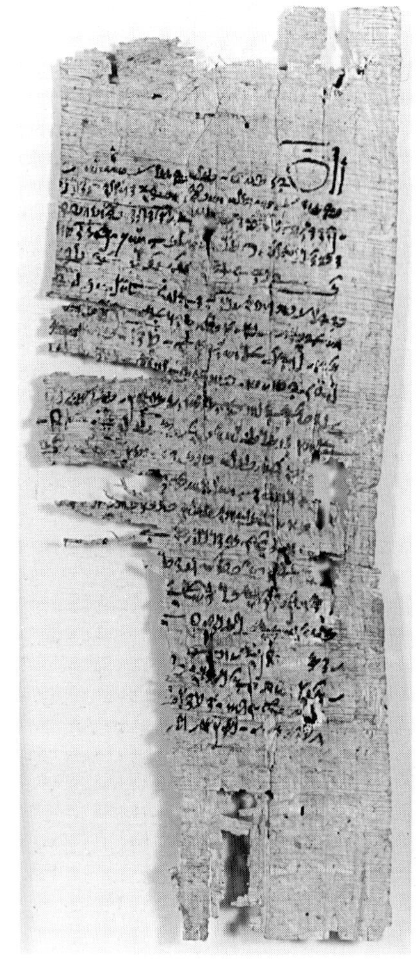

1. (Left) Papyrus: a legal contract of 198/7 BC. (Durham University Oriental Museum, 1952.6.)

2. (Below) An *ostracon*: even important documents such as this tax receipt were written on broken pottery sherds rather than on papyrus; early Roman. (Durham University Oriental Museum, 1951.31.)

we have thousands of documents written by all classes of people down to the totally illiterate who had to dictate to professional scribes and sign them with a cross. It is the story of these people that is presented in this book.

In the United States of America the principal early researcher of the papyri was A. R. Boak of the University of Michigan. Unlike his contemporaries in Europe, he did appreciate the importance of excavating settlements as well as the rubbish dumps that held the majority of the papyri. He published the plans of many buildings at Socnopaiou Nepos and, above all, Karanis. Two preliminary reports were published on Karanis. Major reports were also issued on the papyri (PMich) and the finds of Roman glass (figures 23-4). A substantial part of Karanis was excavated, and it is the only town of Graeco-Roman Egypt for which we have a detailed picture of its overall physical appearance. However, just as the papyri are not exhibited in museums, so the sites they came from are not easy to visit. All archaeological sites in Egypt become covered again by the drifting sands from which they came unless they are continuously maintained.

Apart from a few major temples, the less spectacular Greek and Roman remains do not receive this attention. The geography of Egypt is unique. The Nile forms a life-giving green ribbon flowing through an otherwise inhospitable desert. One of the richest areas for papyri and one of the most densely inhabited areas of Graeco-Roman Egypt was the Fayum, a shallow lake to the south-west of the Nile delta. In the Ptolemaic Period the surrounding irrigation system was greatly extended and a large number of Greek towns were established all around it. These towns included Karanis, Socnopaiou Nepos, Kerkeosiris and Theadelphia. The Fayum continued as a rich agricultural area into the Roman period, but it seems that the irrigation system broke down in late Roman times and the area was not developed in the medieval period.

Beneath the political institutions encouraged by the Greeks and Romans there could always be seen the old Egyptian cultural roots. Almost all the papyri were written in Greek, the *lingua franca* of the classical Middle East, but even there we can see Egyptian names of people and of gods. Hieroglyphs continued to be used through most of the period covered by this book. In Roman times, as a broad generalisation, we can say that Latin was the language of official decrees, Greek was the intellectual language and Egyptian was the everyday language of the street. Though the classical peoples of the rest of the Mediterranean always regarded Egypt as a strange country apart, they could not escape being influenced by Egyptian culture in their own homelands. The study of Graeco-Roman Egypt tell us as much about Greece and Rome as it does about Egypt itself.

3. A cartouche: the hieroglyphic name and titles of Ptolemy V Epiphanes (204-181 BC). (Courtesy of John Ruffle.)

4. Rear wall of the Temple of Hathor, Dendera, begun in the second century BC. The reliefs show Cleopatra presenting her son Caesarion to the gods. The lion-headed drain spouts are an element of Greek architecture introduced into Egypt. (Courtesy of John Ruffle.)

2
History and administration

During the great era when the Greeks established colonies across the Mediterranean their presence in Egypt was strictly controlled by the Pharaohs. The first major Greek intervention in Egyptian history occurred when Psammetichus I (664-610 BC) used Ionian and Carian mercenaries to regain his throne. From then on Greek soldiers took part in many major Egyptian campaigns. During a campaign against Nubia at the end of the sixth century BC they recorded their visit with inscriptions at the temple at Abu Simbel.

The only major Greek town in Egypt before the days of Alexander the Great was Naucratis, which was founded by Ionian colonists from Miletus in the later sixth century BC. Naucratis has been excavated intermittently since the nineteenth century, but much still remains to be learnt about it. Greek traders did set up in other Egyptian towns and occasionally the citizens of Naucratis tried to encourage Egyptian help in Greek affairs. Normally the Egyptians maintained an aloofness which was matched by Greek respect for such an ancient civilisation.

Alexander the Great

Since the days of the most powerful Pharaohs the Egyptians had found themselves in conflict with the powers of Asia Minor and with Persia. They must, however, have watched with incredulity the victories of the new and barbarian power of Macedonia. It is little wonder that they should ascribe to Alexander the Pharaonic power of a god-king.

In characteristic fashion Alexander stayed less than a year after conquering Egypt in 332 BC. During this short time he visited the oracle of Amun at Siwa and founded Alexandria, but we do not know of his other actions in the country.

The Ptolemies

On Alexander's death in 323 BC Egypt was taken over by his general Ptolemy. Ptolemy was quick to take up the reins of the Pharaonic administration and had himself crowned as Ptolemy Soter in 305 BC. He tried to ensure the loyalty of the Egyptian population by setting himself within their ancient religious traditions. The public image of the Ptolemies as inscribed on monuments and set out in official administrative documents was Egyptian (figure 3). Despite this the first Ptolemy and his successors maintained a strong Greek personal identity. They always adopted Greek names and titles and none of them spoke Egyptian until Cleopatra. Greeks were favoured over Egyptians in civil and military functions, and there was often social unrest between the two races.

The Ptolemaic dynasty was very much a family affair characterised by internal squabbles that were resolved by murders, carefully worded treaties and brother-sister marriages. Their ceremonies and luxurious living matched the extravagances of their personal politics.

Ptolemaic possessions abroad included Cyprus and Cyrenaica. The Ptolemies also engaged in a continuous to and fro struggle with the Seleucid rulers of Syria for the control of the eastern Mediterranean coast.

Ptolemaic administration

All the Ptolemaic decrees, even those addressed to the smallest villages, claimed to come personally from the Pharaoh. Although the king's correspondence on such matters was clearly dictated by his ministers, the Ptolemaic civil service gave the central administration more opportunity than most to know the people's actions. It was the *dioiketes,* or minister of finance, who held the strings of power on behalf of the king. Below the level of the chief ministers, the bureaucracy was not divided according to function so much as according to a strict hierarchy of jurisdiction. Orders were passed downwards from the palace concerning every detail of government and city administration.

An idea of the efficiency of the system can be gained from an excerpt of the daily records of the royal post, kept on an hour-to-hour basis.

> 'The 19th, 11th hour, Nicodemus delivered to Alexander ... scrolls from the lower country from King Ptolemy for Antiochus in the Heracleopolite nome; 1 scroll for Demetrius the officer of the Thebaid in charge of the elephant supply; 1 scroll for ...' (PHib 110, 255 BC.)

The administration in theory worked equally well in the other direction, and the humblest peasant was used to addressing petitions directly to the monarch. Most written complaints were answered by the *strategos* of the nome, the district governor, who appended his orders to the letter and passed copies up and down the bureaucracy.

Scrolls containing legal records of court proceedings, land ownership, births and deaths were always passing up the hierarchy of the administration from the office of the village scribe to the central Catalogue, as it was called, of the *archidikastes,* or chief justice, in Alexandria. The Ptolemaic administration was run very much from the bottom up. It was supported by a large number of very thorough and persistent village scribes who made sure that there was a continual stream of paperwork passing up to central government.

The land itself belonged personally to the king and his prime concern was the efficient working of the agricultural system, the repairing of the dykes, the storage of the harvest and the collection of taxes. As is usual in large bureaucracies, the opportunities for corruption were many; jobs were bought and sold. The Greeks brought coinage into Egypt for the first time and there is some evidence that they took advantage of its unfamiliarity to the natives. In later Ptolemaic times posts in the administration became hereditary.

Caesar, Antony and Cleopatra

The end of Ptolemaic Egypt came about in characteristically murderous fashion. Ptolemy XIII, embroiled in a typical dynastic struggle with his sister, Cleopatra VII Thea Philopator, murdered the Roman general Pompey in 48 BC to gain the support of Pompey's rival Caesar. Caesar became very attracted to Cleopatra and she had a son by him, called Caesarion (figure 4). After the murder of Caesar in Rome Mark Antony took over Caesar's political legacy in the east. Cleopatra was pursuing her country's traditional interests by encouraging him to associate with her as well. She probably hoped to gain control of Palestine and Lebanon, in which Ptolemaic rulers and earlier Pharaohs had always claimed an interest. Internal Roman politics, and love, played their part.

The Roman Pharaoh

The Emperor Augustus took to heart the system of the Ptolemies, after his defeat of Antony and Cleopatra at Actium in 31 BC. He decided that Egypt was his personal possession by right of conquest. He was worried that Roman senators would seize the riches of the country and challenge his power. To prevent this, no senator was allowed to visit Egypt without the emperor's permission.

Personal rule allowed Augustus to dispense with the usual form of Roman provincial administration and assume the position previously occupied by the king (figure 5). In Rome Augustus was keen to play down the fact that the Egyptians regarded him as a Pharaoh, and thus a god. After Egyptians had had more contact with the Empire under later emperors this belief probably lapsed.

When Christianity became the state religion in the fourth century AD there seems to have been little personal allegiance to the emperor. From the late fourth century AD Egypt fell under the control of the Byzantine emperor at Constantinople. The person with the most political power within the country at that time was the patriarch, the head of the Egyptian church. The last Byzantine patriarch, Cyrus, led the opposition to the Arabs and negotiated terms of surrender with them when they conquered Egypt in AD 639-42.

5. Augustus as Pharaoh (small figure) faces the gods of Egypt at the Temple of Hathor, Dendera. (Author.)

The Roman administration

Augustus essentially continued the previous system of administration used by the Ptolemies. The 'governor', or rather the personal representative of the emperor, was the Prefect. Under him were the special Roman officials concerned with Roman law (the *iuridicus*) and finance (the *idius logos* and various *procuratores*). Other high officials had roles similar to those of their Greek counterparts and many of them were local people.

In all the provinces of the Roman Empire some effort was put into encouraging cities to run their own local administration. This policy saved the Romans from having to administer the whole Empire themselves. In Britain and France the Romans had difficulties because there was no strong urban tradition. In Egypt there was a very long history of urban settlement but throughout this time towns had been administered by central government. A full network of city councils was not established until the third century AD.

As during the Ptolemaic period, the administration drew most of its income from the agricultural surplus. Whereas, however, in earlier times the grain surplus had been available for open export, in Roman times the state commandeered the surplus to feed the Roman capital and, from the fourth century AD, Constantinople. A special administration, the *annona*, was set up to organise the transport of grain to Rome and its free distribution to those who were entitled. In Ptolemaic times the salaries of the administration were paid out of taxes. In Roman times much of the local administration was carried out by unpaid co-opted 'volunteers', who were expected to be motivated by civic pride, or by contractors, who paid themselves by overtaxing the people.

Egypt was not just the personal property of the Roman emperor; it was also organised so that its economic output helped keep him in power. Its corn went to feed the Roman voters and its mineral wealth went straight into the imperial treasury. The Romans turned round the pre-existing bureaucracy to work for them. The Egyptians might threaten to withhold the grain supply but this was rarely done for fear of the retribution that would surely follow.

3
Settlements

There was a wide range of settlements in Graeco-Roman Egypt. At the top were unique foundations enjoying a special status, such as the early Greek colony of Naucratis, the Greek capital Alexandria and the Emperor Hadrian's special foundation Antinoopolis. Egyptian nomes, or provinces, had been established by New Kingdom times and most of the country was still run from them. The nome capitals were essentially like Graeco-Roman market towns. During the Roman period they developed classical institutions and public buildings. Finally there was a plethora of smaller towns and villages, farms and larger rural estates. We know less about the archaeology of some of these types of settlement than others.

Alexandria

One of the greatest cities of the ancient world, and the most famous of Alexander the Great's new towns, Alexandria was founded in 331 BC. It exerted an enormous cultural and commercial influence right across the Mediterranean until the Arab conquest in the seventh century AD. Alexandria controlled the trade routes to Africa and India. It was the chief port for the exports from the rich Nile valley and the base for the grain fleet that fed Rome. The populace was renowned for its cosmopolitan composition and its propensity to riot.

Like many great cities, Alexandria seemed more important than the country in which it was situated. With its thoroughly Greek culture and complex racial mix, it was like no other place in Egypt. This mix made it a hotbed of political dissent. Citizenship was jealously guarded, even though the city's town council was abolished for unknown reasons during the Ptolemaic Period. Roman emperors were often petitioned for Alexandrian citizenship, though the council was not restored until AD 200. Diodorus Siculus thought that there were 300,000 citizens in the time of Augustus, and the complete population probably numbered almost twice that figure.

Unfortunately very few archaeological traces of the city have been found or published in detail. Nothing is known of the palace of the Ptolemies or the Great Library and Museum. The destruction of the latter buildings by fire, first during the occupation by Caesar and again in the third century AD, is still regretted as an immense loss to classical scholarship. Elements of two great temples, the Ptolemaic Serapeum and the Caesarium, survived until the nineteenth century. Obelisks from the Caesarium, which had been derived from Pharaonic temples, now stand in Central Park, New York, and by the Thames in London. The Pharos lighthouse, one of the Seven Wonders of the World, also of the Ptolemaic Period, has disappeared, although its site is known.

The only major group of surviving buildings was recovered at Kom el-Dik, near the centre of the old city. They all seem to date from the third century AD at the earliest. There are large public baths and an *odeon*, a form of small theatre used for public meetings. A third major building has been identified as a 'school'. It consists of three adjacent long narrow rooms. Each room has tiered stone benches running round the far end and, in the central room, some way down the sides. The similarity in overall structure to a theatre, or *odeon*, does imply a use for public speaking, but there is no firm evidence for the function of the building.

The nome capitals

There was a reduction to about thirty administrative districts, or nomes, in Ptolemaic and Roman Egypt, each with its particular urban centre. Much more is known about these centres from papyri than from any archaeological evidence. The best known is Oxyrhynchus, situated about 80 km south of the Fayum. Oxyrhynchus has produced one of the largest collections of papyri, which are housed in Oxford. These papyri mention around twenty temples, including one dedicated to Serapis, where there was a bank. There were at least four public baths, a *gymnasium* (this was an important political institution in Greek towns and not just an exercise club), a hippodrome and, in the late Roman period, two churches. The remains of the theatre suggest it could have held up to 1000 people, although it is impossible to use this as a basis for calculating the total population. Ancient public buildings were built to be as large and impressive as possible, rather than to seat an audience of

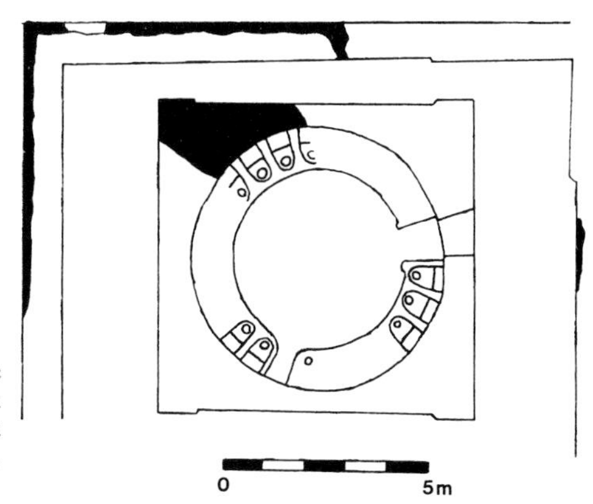

6. Ptolemaic baths from the nome capital of Buto in the Nile delta. A central domed room is ringed by a series of individual footbaths. (Author.)

a certain size. A document of the third century AD records that there were 4000 citizens in Oxyrhynchus. If the population that could not vote is included it would make a total of around 6000.

These towns were medium-sized market towns. There were some forms of classical architecture (figure 6), such as colonnaded streets. The towns do not seem to have been the kind of regularly planned settlement found elsewhere in the classical Mediterranean world. Since many of them were founded in Pharaonic times it was difficult for them to adapt their urban structure to the new Greek model.

Villages

Villages form the best known group of settlements from Graeco-Roman Egypt. Many early excavations encountered small groups of late Roman or Byzantine houses which had been built inside the earlier Pharaonic temples that they were investigating. Some larger villages were investigated in detail during the first half of the twentieth century.

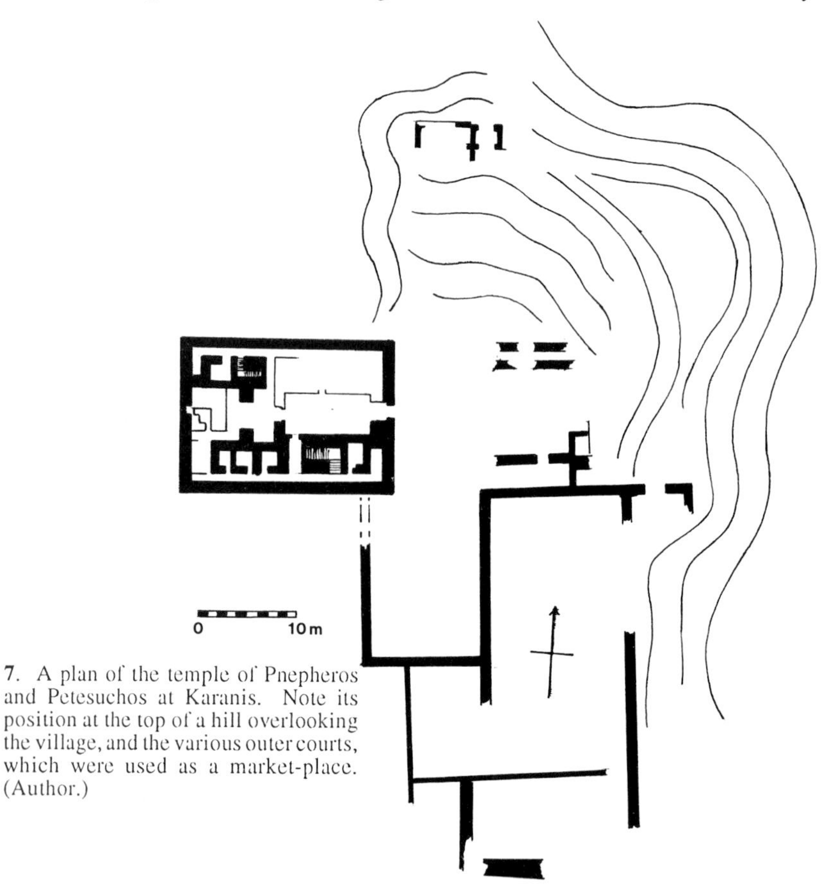

7. A plan of the temple of Pnepheros and Petesuchos at Karanis. Note its position at the top of a hill overlooking the village, and the various outer courts, which were used as a market-place. (Author.)

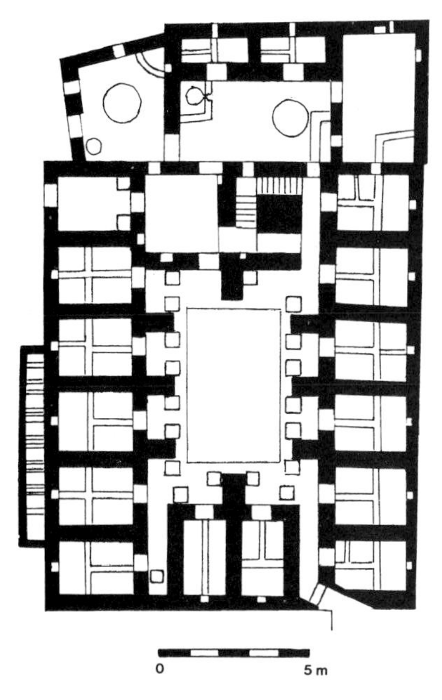

8. Ground-floor plan of granary C65 at Karanis; late Roman period. (Author.)

The village or small town or Karanis in the Fayum is the only settlement of Roman Egypt which has been extensively excavated, from which we have large numbers of papyri and which has been published in great detail. As with the nome capitals, major temples (figure 7) determined the overall urban form.

There were at least seven granaries in the town, several of which were so large as to imply a public function (figure 8). They consisted of ranges of storerooms, each 3 by 2 metres in size, around a central courtyard. The largest granary (C65) measured 18.5 by 16 metres and was 10 metres, or three storeys, high. Inside it there were 42 storerooms, each one divided into four compartments. Two yards on one side of the building contained settings for large millstones. Like all the buildings in Karanis other than the main temples, the granaries were constructed from mudbrick, with wooden planks for door and window frames. Next to the very large granary (C65) was a long narrow building 16 metres wide and 32.5 metres long. Its courtyard extended a further 19.5 metres in the same direction. Many *ostraca* (figure 2) recording the transport of grain were found in the building, and it may have been the barracks for soldiers guarding the granary.

Karanis has produced no evidence for baths or the other public buildings found in larger towns. Nevertheless Karanis was still an urban settlement. There were some open spaces within the town, but it was generally full of dense housing in rectangular blocks. The two or three main streets were 3-4 metres wide and minor streets were about 1 metre wide. The streets did not run directly across the town but had to zigzag around the irregularly positioned street blocks.

The tax registers of Karanis for AD 172-3 list 1000 citizens. This, it is generally agreed, is likely to represent a total population of about 5000, allowing for those who were disenfranchised or exempt from taxation for some reason. Many villages were much smaller than Karanis and consisted of only a few houses.

Estates

From the earliest times Egyptian aristocrats held large rural possessions but during the Roman period we have considerable numbers of papyri concerned with the administration of large estates by bailiffs. The estate administration could be a complex bureaucracy in its own right. The estate of the Apion family, who rose to high office at the Byzantine court, had a hierarchy of managers to cover various districts. Careful organisation was needed to collect the harvest and the rent from a range of widely dispersed holdings.

No rural estates have been excavated, although some small villages might have been part of estates. One would like to know whether the main estate of the aristocrat included the form of Roman villa which is familiar in the northern part of the Roman Empire. It is possible that the conventional form of Roman villa did not exist in Egypt. As we shall see in the next chapter, Egyptian town houses were very different to normal Roman ones.

Urban life

Urban life has always involved social and civic obligations to make sure that the settlement ran efficiently. Aristocrats and villagers were often co-opted into forced labour. There were hundreds of duties: supervising agricultural activities, organising festivals and visits of important people, looking after public money and the construction of public buildings. Most contentious of all was the collection of taxes. Where money could be made by corruption, for example by overtaxing people and pocketing the surplus, there were many people eager to take up the job, but if the job was likely to leave the official out of pocket then someone had to be forced to take it on.

An example of the kind of dispute that could arise is the complaint of a tax-collector in 23 BC:

> 'To Asclepiades, nomarch, from Nechembes. After I had contracted for the tax of the sixth for Arsinoe Philadelphus in the division of Heracleides for the tenth year, there was an incursion

of locusts which destroyed everything, what was saved being carried off by the owners without payment of the sixth.' (PTebt 772.)

Everyone seems to have taken out loans, borrowing from those of a higher class with money, and lending to those of similar or inferior status to themselves. Wherever there was spare cash it could be loaned at high rates of interest: 12 per cent on cash loans and a remarkable 50 per cent for loans against seed or crops. The vagaries of the Nile's annual flood probably account for the pervasive nature of loans in Egypt. Fortunes were made or lost on success in agriculture, depending on whether the Nile was beneficial or disastrous. Either way, a farmer had to gamble.

Financial and social obligations thus extended up and down Egyptian society, knitting together villager and townsman. We often think of ancient society as consisting of peasant farmers, who were most concerned about the best weather for their crops. In Egypt there was a complex financial system of loan and credit, not far removed from present-day obligations.

9. Small painted palette showing a tailor or a barber in his shop. Hawara; Roman. (Trustees of the National Museums of Scotland, 1911.210.4.G.)

There were other financial dangers as well. In AD 28 a villager reported to the police that a builder had robbed him during alterations to his house. The builder took away a box of jewellery that the owner's mother had hidden 43 years earlier. In another incident, in AD 176, the robbers broke in by removing the nails from the front door while the house owner was away for a funeral. In one city block in Karanis 25 hoards were found, totalling around 27,000 coins, all dating to before the fourth century AD. Money was often hidden in pots or bags in the mud floor of a room, but in one house four hoards were simply piled against the wall of the cellar. Most crimes were punished by fines, but more serious offenders could be given hard labour in the quarries.

Against the problems of urban life should be set the advantages, such as better services like shops (figure 9), education, entertainment medicine and access to officials.

Demographic change

The populations of these settlements reached their greatest extent in the second century AD. After this date their populations began to fall. In the second century AD Karanis had about 5000 inhabitants in an area of about 125,000 square metres. By the end of the third century the population had fallen to less than 500. By the end of the fourth century there were very few people left in the village at all. Similar stories come from other villages. Even in a nome capital like Oxyrhynchus a late third-century papyrus (POsl 111) records that 40 per cent of houses in one district had been abandoned. Explanations range from a plague in the late second century AD to agricultural decline and encroachment by the desert in the late Roman times.

Throughout their existence the Egyptian settlements had problems with drifting sand. It was normal for townspeople to abandon the lower storeys of their buildings, which filled with sand, so that the first floor became the new ground floor, and another new storey was added to the roof. Street surfaces had to be raised periodically as well. At Karanis there were approximately seven broad changes of level, which form the basis for the dating sequence of the site.

It is difficult to accept that Egyptian communities whose whole existence depended on controlling and farming the desert would let the dunes get the better of them in this way. Sand seems to have been filling the buildings when the towns were prosperous and expanding in the early Roman period. Archaeologists have become more and more sceptical of attributing population decline to sudden disasters. It is likely that behind these developments is some form of long-term social and perhaps environmental change, which we only partly understand at present.

4
Domestic life

Housing

We know a considerable amount about Egyptian housing from papyri that record sales and leases of property. By and large this accords well with what we know of their form from archaeology. Most Egyptians of the Greek and Roman period, even if they lived in small villages, inhabited communities of densely packed housing. While individual houses clearly did exist in many places, most townspeople lived in apartment blocks that were two or more storeys high (figures 10 and 11).

The houses were built with standard-sized mudbricks (25 by 10 by 10 cm at Karanis). The walls tapered to support the enormous weight. They might be 2 metres thick at ground level and 25-30 cm thick at roof level. Additional stability was provided by timber framing within the walls. Where the building was subject to wear or needed strength, such as thresholds, steps and at the corners of the house, stones or fired bricks were used. Windows were made with wooden frames 1 metre tall and 50 cm wide. They were divided by wooden bars or shutters but had no glass. Doors were made of wooden planks. They were closed with a variety of latch fastenings that needed special keys to open them. The houses usually had cellars which were barrel-vaulted in mudbrick, but upper floors were made by placing straw matting and mud over wooden rafters.

At Karanis the interior walls of the rooms were covered with a strange black wash, and the courses of mudbrick were outlined with white lines. The only place in the houses where there was any significant decoration was in the niches (figure 12) that are found in the walls of some of the larger rooms. Some had high relief decoration in stucco with a variety of geometric designs. Others had small crude paintings of minor gods, from which it is concluded that they were household shrines. A late Roman apartment block in Alexandria had a large figure of the Virgin painted on the wall of a courtyard.

House sales and leases allow us to generalise on the way rooms were distributed within the houses. Houses were organised around a square staircase with a central pillar. All the rooms opened on to this stair. Dining rooms and bedrooms were always found on upper floors. One papyrus (PLond V, 1722, AD 573) mentions two open-air dining rooms, which were presumably on the roof. Reception or living rooms could be found on any floor from the ground up. The papyri also mention *atria*, but provincial Roman houses hardly ever had these Pompeian-style colonnaded reception rooms and there is no archaeological evi-

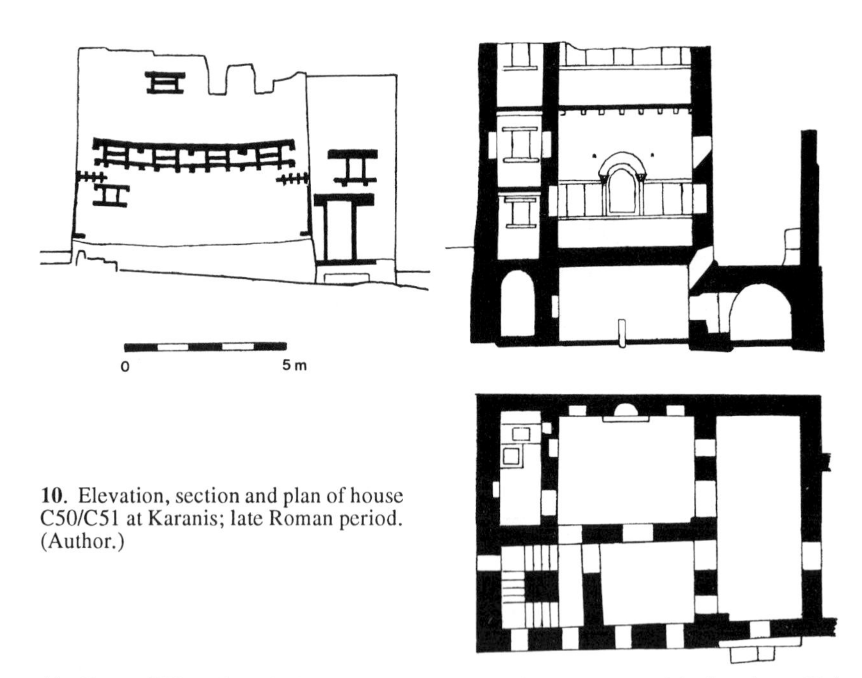

10. Elevation, section and plan of house C50/C51 at Karanis; late Roman period. (Author.)

11. House C68 at Karanis; late Roman period. (Kelsey Museum of Archaeology, University of Michigan.)

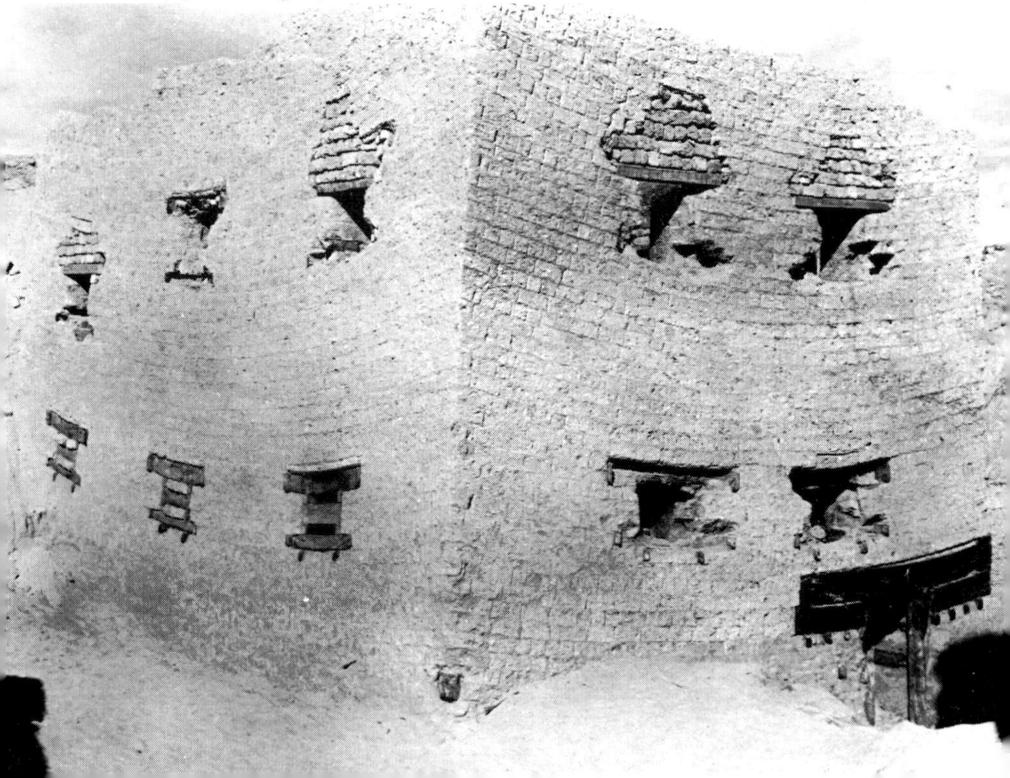

12. Niche decorated with moulded stucco. House C71, Karanis; late Roman period. (Kelsey Museum of Archaeology, University of Michigan.)

dence for this kind of room in Egypt. The term may reflect the function of the room rather than any specific architectural form. All the rooms were usually 3.5 by 2.5 metres in plan without any architectural distinction, so that their functions were interchangeable. Occasionally bigger houses had a larger, better decorated room, which was presumably a purpose-built reception suite, but this is rare. Otherwise the only architectural distinction between rooms was the occasional cupboard built into the wall. These were normally about 1 metre high, 50 cm wide and 30 cm deep.

Furniture

A papyrus of AD 200 (PStPal XX, 67) gives a list of furniture in a house. In the basement we find a lamp and stand of bronze, various cups and saucers, a spare cloak and a blanket, the bath and a basin. Upstairs there is the kitchen equipment — a colander, mixing bowls, knives, measures — and two mattresses, two pillows, three blankets, one couch, one chest and three cloaks. In those times people ate whilst reclining on one elbow, so the couch could have been used for the living room, the dining room or the spare bedroom. In poor houses or apartments a single room would have fulfilled all these roles anyway. A marble table suitable for use with a dining couch was found in an apartment block of Roman Alexandria. An inventory of furniture in a richer seventh-century AD dining room (POxy 1925) includes dining couches, folding wooden screens, two icons and a shield, which might

13. Small decorated wooden box from Karanis; found in the ground floor of the house shown in figure 10. (Kelsey Museum of Archaeology, University of Michigan, KM 54837.)

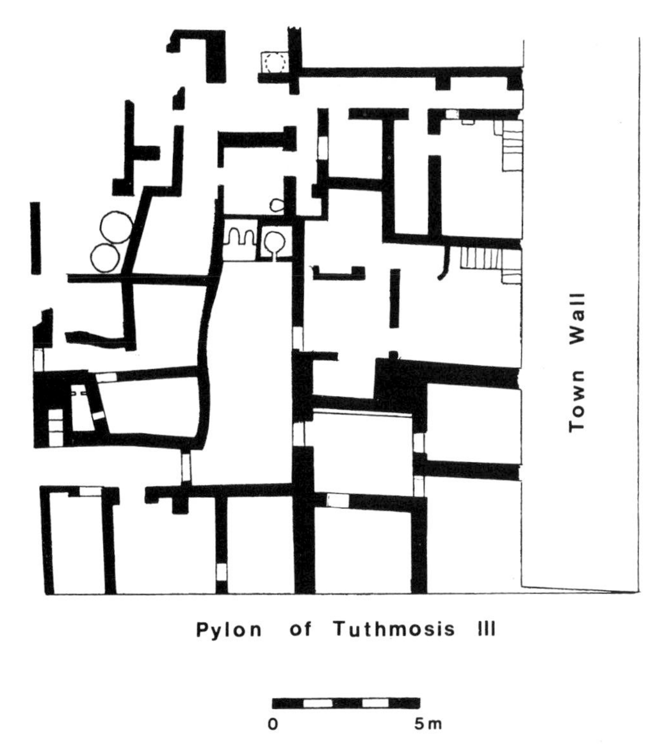

14. Houses of late Roman to Arab period, built in the precinct of the Pharaonic temple at Armant. Note the central courtyard and ovens. (Author.)

have been a souvenir from military service or a hunting trophy. Poor provincials would have used low wooden tables or eaten off the floor. Mattresses could be rolled up for storage in a chest or used for sitting on the floor, as in traditional Middle Eastern houses today.

Lighting was by oil lamps. Through the Greek and early Roman period they were made of pottery and had the familiar form of an enclosed bowl with a protruding beak to take the wick (figure 25). From the late Roman times they were often made of bronze or consisted of conical glass cups (figure 23). Several such lamps could be grouped together in a kind of candelabrum of bronze to light a large room. One lamp would be left in a small niche near the doorway, where we would expect to find the light switch. It would be lit on entry to the room and then used to light the others.

Another niche lay close to the front door and contained a medium-sized pottery jug. Early excavators argued that this demonstrated the

15. Small wicker basket from Hawara; Roman period. Baskets could be used at home or at work, for storage or carrying goods. (Courtesy of the Petrie Museum of Egyptian Archaeology, University College London, UC28047.)

existence of another traditional modern Middle Eastern habit. The jug would be full of water and was available to visitors and passers-by as a mark of hospitality. Some of the houses at Karanis had the occasional amphora (figure 26) in a downstairs room. These large pottery jars were originally used for wine or olive oil by their manufacturers but they were often reused for general household storage.

Cooking was too dangerous and smoky to take place indoors. Sales and leases often tell of having a share in the upkeep of the communal oven, which was located in the court shared by all the apartments (figure 14). Two or three ovens and a quernstone for grinding corn would be placed together here.

The cheapest everyday utensils were made of wood or pottery. Woven baskets are commonly found on excavations in the dry sand of Egypt (figure 15). Glass may have been more expensive than pottery, although in late Roman times it became freely available. Metal items were the most expensive and highly valued by their owners. Stone containers varied in value from the routine mixing bowl, or *mortarium*, for grinding food, to the expensive marble table mentioned earlier.

Family life

As in most societies, the house was the most important asset that was owned by a family. Whilst most other traditional societies pass on property intact to the eldest child, the Egyptians divided it equally among all the children including daughters. As daughters married, parts of a property passed out of the hands of the original family and were further split up by their children. The most extreme case (BGU

115) of this kind gives seventeen adults and three children owning one-tenth of a house! Most of these people were relatives. Clearly not everyone in this group could have enforced their right to live in the family home, but many Egyptian houses were very crowded. Some papyri mention rooms that were unavailable as they were occupied by some stranger, or perhaps a distant relative. The largest known apartment block at Karanis had 45 rooms and must have become split into many flats.

There cannot have been much privacy in these houses. All rooms opened on to the same staircase giving access to the enclosed courtyard. The yard itself was shared by all the apartments. It was used for cooking, washing, and to shelter chickens or a goat.

Women married at the age of thirteen or fourteen, when their husbands were about five years older. There were a number of brother and sister marriages which we would find incestuous. In traditional societies forms of marriage are closely related to the inheritance of wealth and rank. In Egypt these marriages may have been a way of offsetting the problems caused by the equal division of property. Divorce does not seem to have been difficult if the relationship did not work. In one instance from the second century BC, a man, Totoes, divorced his wife, Tareesis, and married her younger sister Takmeis, who was fifteen to twenty years his junior. Tareesis later remarried, her new husband being Totoes' younger brother Horus! While the circumstances behind these events remain unknown, they would have kept the two families united and prevented the dispersal of property.

In these dealings women do not always come off worst. In the late sixth century AD Mary of Syene owned a half share of two rooms, which she divided equally between three sons and one daughter. Her daughter, Tapia, bought out one brother. In AD 585 (PMon 9) Tapia sold her property to her son-in-law and then in AD 594 (PLond V, 1733) sold it again to a soldier! The later papyrus was found amongst the documents of her son-in-law. Either Tapia was a clever lawyer or the deal with the soldier fell through!

Food

Most Egyptians followed a diet that consisted for the most part of vegetables and grain. The vegetables would be eaten raw as a salad, or in some form of soup. They did eat some meat, usually chicken, and fish from the Nile was important. Fishing was sometimes on an industrial scale, with private breeding ponds. Excavations sometimes find 2000-year-old loaves preserved in the hot sands (figure 16). These seem to have been the flat disc-shaped bread most common in the Middle East today. Olive oil for sauces and wine for drinking were available in both local and imported varieties. Beer was often drunk as well. The seventh-century AD Archbishop of Alexandria, John the Almsgiver, modestly turned down imported Palestinian wine (figure 26) in favour of a local vintage, which he said was cheap and had a taste to match its price. John was also offered honey from North Africa. Honey was used as a sweetener in ancient times since raw sugar was not known. Rich Alexandrians from the fourth century BC onwards could always expect to pick up such luxurious titbits that were brought in by the merchants.

16. Bread found preserved in one of the granaries at Karanis; late Roman period. (Kelsey Museum of Archaeology, University of Michigan.)

5
Economic life

Agriculture and the Nile were the dominant forces in the economic life of Greek and Roman Egypt. In this chapter we will look at Egyptian farming and at a number of other crafts and industries for which Egypt became famous in ancient times.

Agriculture

The annual flooding of the Nile, in July to August, and the rich alluvial soil that this brought, were vital to the prosperity of Egypt. Pliny the Elder (*Natural History*, 5, 58) tells us that an inundation of 5.5 metres left the country starving, whilst 7 metres gave a bumper harvest. Nilometers were constructed to measure the height of the water. They consisted of a pole or rock marked with gradations, or sometimes they were formed from a deep wide well near the river bank. The measurements were used to calculate the harvest, and hence the level of taxation.

The Ptolemies elaborated and extended the original Egyptian irrigation systems to ensure large agricultural returns. The Romans also enhanced the system. The huge state granaries, familiar from the story of Joseph in the Bible in a much earlier period, were used to provide the *annona*, the free bread dole in the city of Rome. The grain fleet set sail for Italy after every harvest. Relations between Romans and Egyptians depended on the size of the cargo and a safe sea crossing.

The agricultural calendar was controlled by the river (figure 17). From October through the winter, when the river was low, dykes were repaired and seeds sown. All land was owned in small parcels, let and sublet to peasant tenants. They had to borrow seed from the owners in return for part of the crop at the end of the season. The interest level on such loans was 50 per cent, reflecting the uncertainties of the flood.

In addition, the landowners, of whom the most important was the Pharaoh (the Greek king or Roman emperor), imposed forced labour on the peasants. During the winter they each had to spend five days repairing the irrigation system or moving a certain amount of earth. After the harvest had been collected and the landlord had received his share the peasants had to help transport the grain to the river bank for shipping to Alexandria.

The harvest was the most critical time for the whole operation. The papyri are full of complaints about fields of cereal destroyed by neighbours' animals. Full-time guards had to be employed to supervise the threshing, preventing theft at night, making sure that landlords and perhaps tenants received their share.

For all our detailed knowledge of Egypt, surprisingly we have no direct evidence for the yield of cereal crops. A return of more than ten times the grain sown best fits what evidence we have, but the argument is too complex to present here. Exceptional inundations would produce well beyond this estimate.

A detailed study by Crawford of the village of Kerkeosiris in the Ptolemaic Period has shown how much land was given over to different crops. It seems that 50 per cent of the land was under wheat, 2-16 per cent under barley and 13-20 per cent covered with lentils, the biggest non-cereal food crop. Beans, cumin, fenugreek and garlic were also grown at the village. Other cash crops known elsewhere included papyrus and olives.

The most important animal was the sheep. Several people are recorded owning over one thousand animals. The flocks were shorn twice every year. Sheep's and goats' milk cheese was favoured over that made from cows' milk. Traditionally the Egyptian religion, like Judaism, banned the consumption of pork. Chickens and pigeons were very popular. At Karanis there were several large dovecotes (figure 18). Pigeon dung was thought to be the best fertiliser, and some contracts state that tenants must use it.

17. The Nile valley today. (Courtesy of Christine Thompson.)

18. Dovecote C91A/B at Karanis; late Roman period. (Kelsey Museum of Archaeology, University of Michigan.)

The soldier and the economy

The Ptolemaic kings established the system of cleruchy, in which soldiers were given land in return for military service. At Kerkeosiris in 118 BC 33 per cent of the land was owned by cleruchs. At first the army was restricted to Greeks; later it became open to native Egyptians. Officially the land reverted to the Pharaoh on the death of the cleruch, but the soldiers began to bring their sons into the tenancies, until by the first century BC such properties became fully heritable. When the troops were called up and on the move they had to be billeted with the local population, who naturally resented this. Sometimes rather extreme measures were taken:

> 'Memo to Aphthonetos, *strategos*, from Andronicos. We discovered in Crocodilopolis that some of the houses which had been used for billeting have had their roofs removed. The owners have also blocked up the front doors and built altars against them, so that the houses cannot be used for billeting.' (PPetr II. 12 241 BC.)

In the Roman period two legions were based in Alexandria, and a large number of less regular troops were stationed elsewhere. Roman

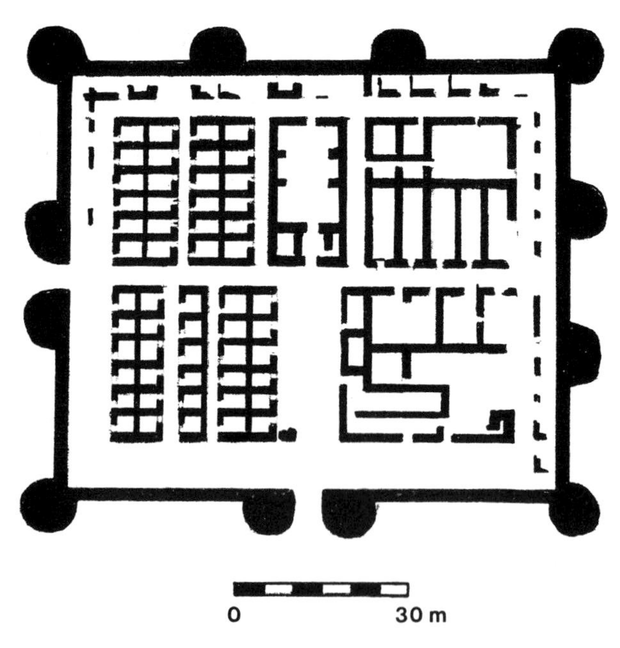

19. Plan of the late Roman fort at Abu Sha'ar on the Red Sea. (Author.)

troops never served in their home province, so the soldiers in Egypt were originally foreigners, while Egyptians served abroad. However, as in Ptolemaic times, there were mixed marriages and local recruitment took place. Only on discharge, after 25 years of service, did the Roman soldier expect to take up the agricultural life. The veteran was often an important local figure because of the influence of his Roman citizenship and the wealth of his saved pay.

Sometimes soldiers might find difficulty in adjusting to civilian life, as this letter from Karanis suggests:

> 'I commend to you the bearer of this letter, Terentianus, an honourably discharged soldier. Explain the customs of our village to him so he isn't insulted.' (SB 9636 AD 136.)

In peacetime Roman soldiers contributed to the economic effort of the country by helping to collect taxes and guarding the transport of grain or minerals. The Eastern Desert was rich in minerals, including the famous stone quarries of Mons Porphyritus and Mons Claudianus. The quarries were worked by slaves or criminals under a private contractor, closely watched by the army. Excavations in 1987-9 at Mons Claudianus by European archaeologists have found material dating from the late first to second centuries AD. They have found no sign of the late Roman occupation, when it was thought that the size of the fort was reduced. On the other hand, American excavations since 1987 at the fort of Abu Sha'ar on the Red Sea coast (figure 19) have found material from the fifth to seventh centuries AD. The withy ceilings of the military buildings had collapsed on the ground after the fort was abandoned. There is a wealth of new investigation to undertake here on the pattern of the military occupation that secured the water supply and trade routes across the desert to the ports that brought in exotic products from India.

Textiles

Tapestries (figure 20) were used to decorate the walls and perhaps the floors of many large buildings. Though the techniques had been known for a long time, most of the examples that survive today date from the late Roman period. Some were used in early churches and show saints or worshippers under architectural façades. They all use strong bright colours, which remain very striking in museums.

The second group of Egyptian textiles is that of dress. Several plain 'shirts' are known from earlier periods. In Roman times it became the

20. Rug of the third to fourth centuries AD, with a colourful border of various fruits, including fig and pomegranate. (Whitworth Art Gallery, University of Manchester, MM 382.1968.)

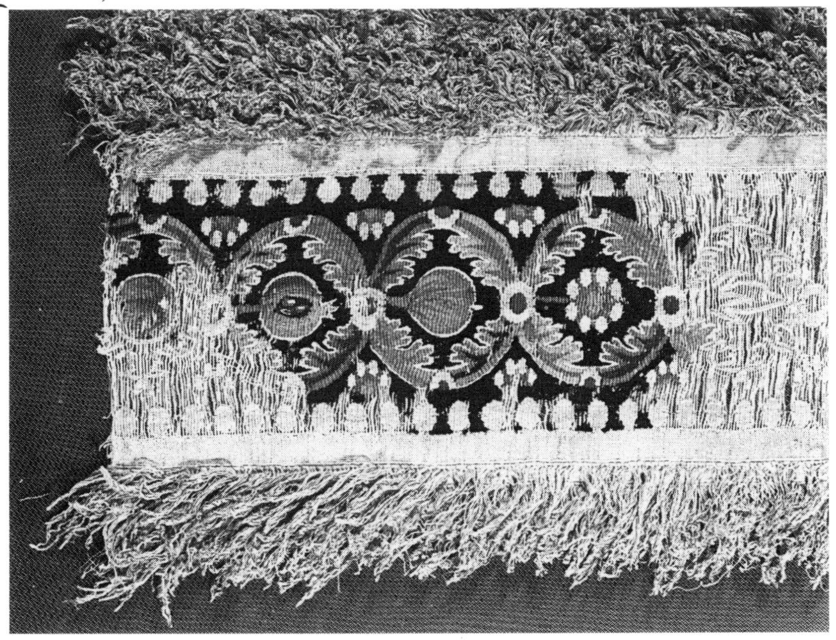

21. Tunic of the fourth to fifth centuries AD, from the nome capital of Panopolis. (Trustees of the Victoria and Albert Museum, 257.1890.)

22. Woven roundel for attachment to a tunic; fourth century AD. (Whitworth Art Gallery, University of Manchester, MW 18395.)

fashion to sew richly coloured strips from the top of the shoulder down to the waist. Decorated medallions of material might be sewn on to the shoulders or the waist. These attachments show lively scenes of cupids swimming, fishing or hunting, surrounded by an array of wildlife and plants (figures 21 and 22). Another common scene on such roundels shows two soldiers or hunters, on horseback, confronting each other.

The richness of Egyptian textiles was well known in the ancient world and many of them found their way to the west, where they have been discovered wrapped round the bones of early saints. The majority of textiles that have been found in Egypt were excavated at the sites of Antinoopolis and Panopolis (Akhmim). It has been suggested that there were important mills at these two towns during the late Roman period.

There have been attempts to construct stylistic chronologies of the textiles, based on a transition from the realistic monochrome designs to less realistic colour depictions. It is hard to be certain about such distinctions since few of the textiles are independently dated.

Glass (figures 23 and 24)

Pharaonic Egypt played a large part in the invention of the techniques of glassworking. After the foundation of Alexandria many important glass workshops became established there, and they maintained a strong trade in glass until the end of the ancient world. The scientific excavation of one of these workshops would be of enormous value to Mediterranean archaeology.

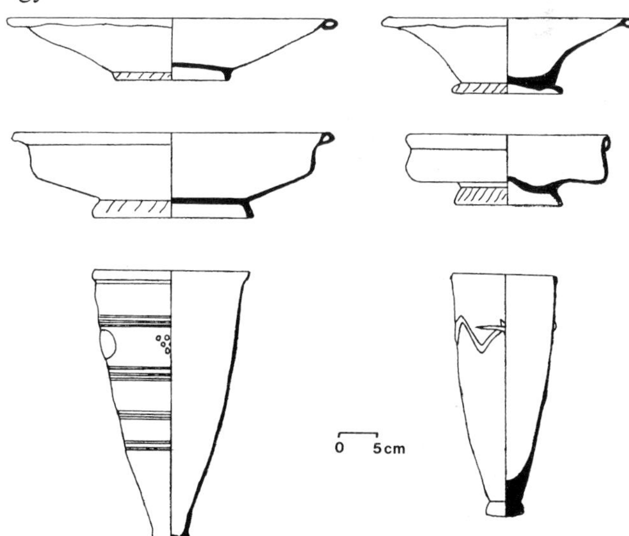

23. Typical forms of Egyptian glass found at Karanis; late Roman period. (Author.)

24. Head of a glass still, used to produce liquor. Roman period. (Courtesy of the Petrie Museum of Egyptian Archaeology, University College London, UC22032.)

During Ptolemaic times the Egyptians produced moulded bowls and were among the leading glassworkers in the world. They helped develop new techniques such as millefiori, where many coloured rods are placed together to create a rainbow-like effect, and gold sandwich glass, where gold foil is cut into patterns and sandwiched between two layers of glass.

Some time in the first century BC the technique of glass-blowing was invented, perhaps in Egypt. The Romans in the west adopted large-scale glass-blowing and raised production to a point where it could compete with pottery for many domestic articles. From late Ptolemaic times the Egyptians had had great success with highly polished bowls and beakers decorated with cut-glass techniques and did not use glass-blowing very much until the late Roman period.

Pottery

There are no modern compendia of Egyptian pottery of the Graeco-Roman period so a general picture must be composed from a variety of site reports and specialist publications.

With the coming of Alexander the Great Egypt joined a unified market covering much of the Mediterranean. Alexandria imported all the fine wares of the day, such as the red-slipped moulded 'Megaran' bowls, and produced its own versions of fine tablewares. Away from the capital and the main Greek settlements local pottery from the Nile valley clays continued to dominate the market as it always had done.

In Roman times there was a similar pattern of trade. In Alexandria

25. A typical Egyptian frog lamp. The frog was a symbol of renewal. The lamp bears an inscription 'To abbot Timothy, archbishop'. This probably refers to either Timothy 'The Cat' or Timothy 'White Hat', rival patriarchs of Alexandria AD 457-82. (Durham University Oriental Museum, 2011.)

traders imported red-slipped dishes from Cyprus, North Africa and Syria. Amphorae containing wine or olive oil were brought in from Antioch in Syria and Gaza in Palestine.

In the fourth century AD the Egyptians produced their own red-slipped tablewares. The main centres of production were probably located at Luxor and the Fayum. Another very common local product was a white-slipped ware decorated with rough designs in dark red slip.

Pottery kilns excavated by a German team near the sanctuary of St Menas, not far west of Alexandria, specialised in the production of

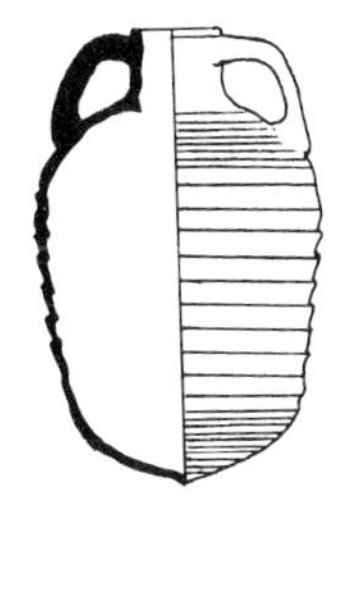

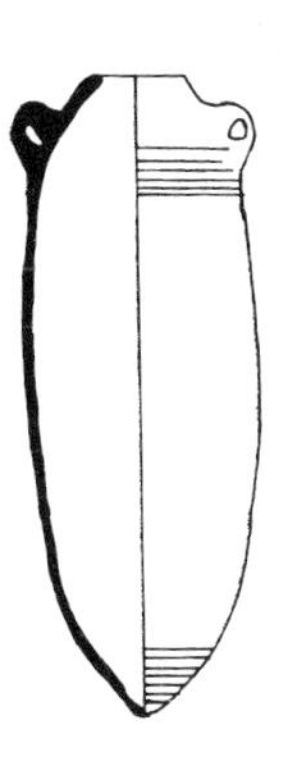

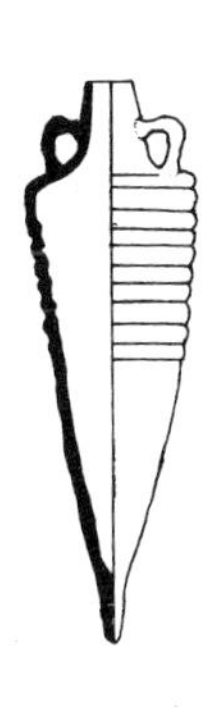

26. Types of amphorae used by the monks of Kellia. They are, from left to right, oil from Antioch in Syria, wine from Gaza in Palestine, and local wine or oil, perhaps from Antinoopolis. (Author.)

27. (Left) Fineware flask in black clay, from Memphis; late Roman period. Flasks of this kind are often called 'pilgrim' flasks, but this example shows no evidence of association with a cult. (Courtesy of the Petrie Museum of Egyptian Archaeology, University College London, UC33329.)

28. (Right) Small terracotta of Harpocrates, from Memphis. Small terracottas were produced in large numbers throughout the Roman period. (Courtesy of the Petrie Museum of Egyptian Archaeology, University College London, UC8760.)

moulded pilgrim flasks which were used for sanctified oil. These souvenirs spread throughout the Mediterranean, and a notable group is preserved at Monza Cathedral in Italy. They are decorated with a scene of one of the more notable miracles of St Menas — strangling two camels simultaneously! The kilns also produced spherical amphorae, and jugs in a white fabric with deeply incised grooves.

In Byzantine times a local type of amphora (figure 26), only 1 metre high, in a dark brown/orange clay began to be exported around the Mediterranean in large numbers. It may have been produced in central Egypt near the town of Antinoopolis.

A particular kind of pottery for which Egypt was well known in the ancient world was the terracotta figurine. This originated in Pharaonic times but in the Graeco-Roman period the repertoire was extended to cover a huge range of minor deities, secular figures and animals. These figurines are found in large numbers throughout the Mediterranean. Many were produced in local kilns, but a good percentage of them are of Egyptian origin.

6
Religion

Throughout the classical period until the advent of Christianity Egyptians continued to worship their old gods in substantially the same way they had always done. The Greeks and the Romans tended to assimilate their gods with those of the natives in varying degrees. Very often it was just a matter of putting a Greek or Latin name to a local god, whose worship would otherwise remain unchanged.

During Ptolemaic times Egyptian cults spread throughout the Greek world. Ptolemy I deliberately encouraged the growth of the cult of Serapis, which was carefully adapted from the cult of Osiris to suit Greek tastes. It was used as an element of foreign policy to spread Egyptian culture. In the wake of Serapis, the cult of Isis gained many converts in Greece and later in Italy. The development of these cults in some ways reflects the influence of classical Greece and Rome on native Egyptian religion, but the Greek adaptations were not meant for the native Egyptian. In the Ptolemaic period there are no records of Greeks serving as priests in native Egyptian cults. The cults of Serapis and Isis were meant to extend the influence of Egyptian culture abroad and were very successful in this. Native Egyptian culture thus had a profound influence on classical Greece and Rome, as well as suffering the impositions of Greek and Roman occupation.

Temples and shrines

Every town in Egypt had its major temples. Their form remained little changed since Pharaonic times. The introduction by the Greeks of the arch allowed a major advance in construction techniques. The temples consisted of a succession of enclosed courts entered by monumental gateways called 'pylons' (figures 7 and 29), which were an Egyptian architectural feature representing the mountains of the horizon. Each court had a different level of sanctity, leading to the sanctuary itself, and access was accordingly restricted. Each Egyptian god was associated with a particular animal and areas in each temple were typically set aside for the burial of thousands of ibis, crocodiles, baboons or other animals.

The outer courts of the temples appear to have resembled a separate village with shops, banks and houses. In 114 BC a tax-collector in Kerkeosiris, named Apollodorus, tried to seize some illicit oil from a house inside a temple (PTebt 39), which presumably belonged to one of the officials or priests there. The tax-collector was beaten and thrown out of the temple. When he later tried to seize the offender in the street,

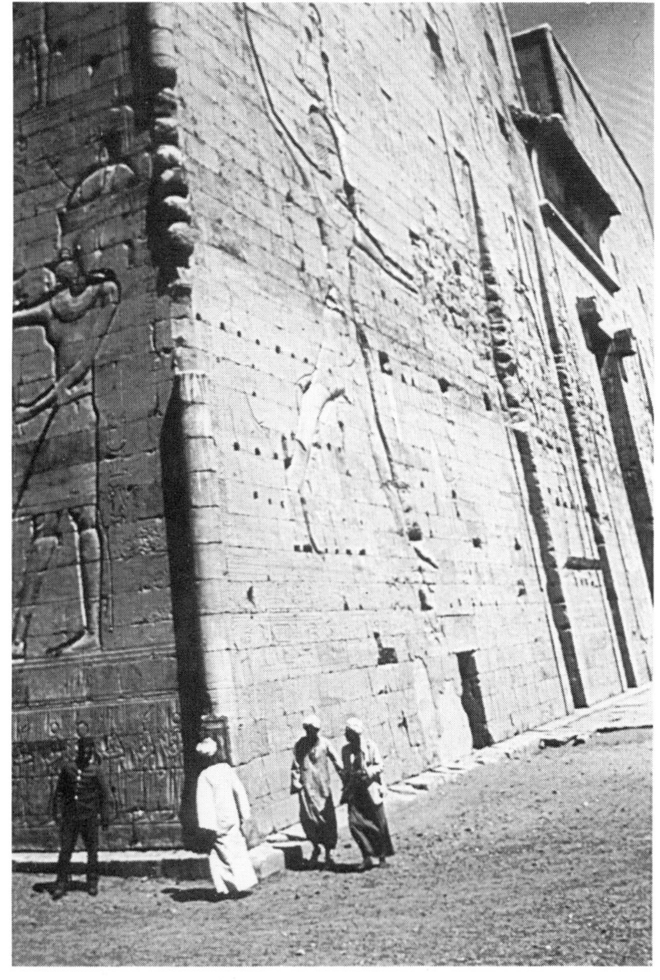

29. Pylon of the Temple of Horus at Apollinopolis Magna (Edfu); third century BC. (Courtesy of John Ruffle.)

both he and his wife were injured.

One of the most important sanctuaries in Egypt was the island of Philae (figures 30, 31, 32) in the middle of the Nile at the First Cataract. The island of Biga to the west of Philae had always been known as the site of Osiris' tomb, and Philae rose to pre-eminence during the classical period as the centre of the cult of Isis. The existing remains include structures built by Ptolemy Philadelphus, Ptolemy Euergetes, Augustus, Hadrian and Diocletian. In the Ptolemaic Period a new annual ceremony was introduced in which the statues of gods were carried to roof chapels where they could be re-animated by the rays of the sun god Re. Such chapels have been found at Philae and Dendera.

The buildings of Philae were flooded by the construction of the Aswan High Dam in the 1960s. They have been relocated to the nearby island of Agilkia, where they now form the most important tourist site of Graeco-Roman Egypt. In ancient times they were also a major tourist attraction, as evidenced by the graffiti of many Roman visitors, including the Emperor Hadrian.

The temples were very powerful institutions within small towns and villages. They employed a large staff. They were the most prominent buildings in the town and were major economic and social centres.

Every house usually had its own shrine. They took the form of arched niches that were decorated with stucco or painted figures. The niches were located in a main reception room or in the yard. Prayers were probably said there throughout the day to protect the household and to give thanks for success.

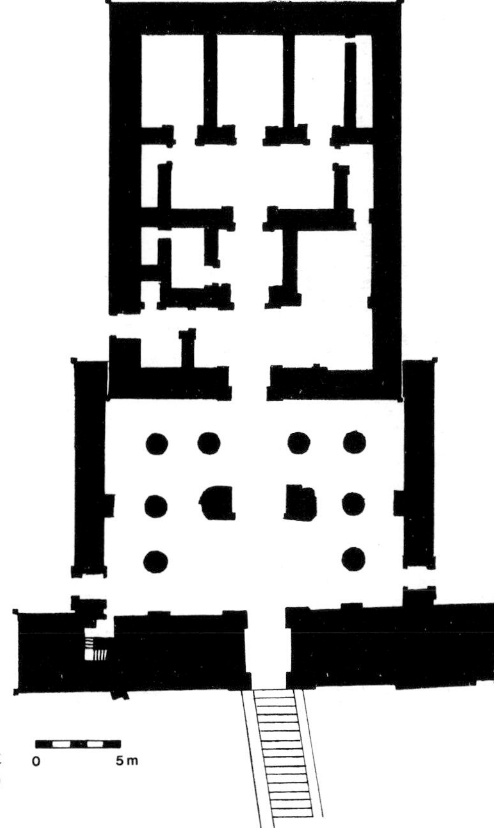

30. Plan of the Temple of Isis at Philae; third century BC. (Author.)

31. Forecourt of the Temple of Isis at Philae from the exterior. (Courtesy of Christine Thompson.)

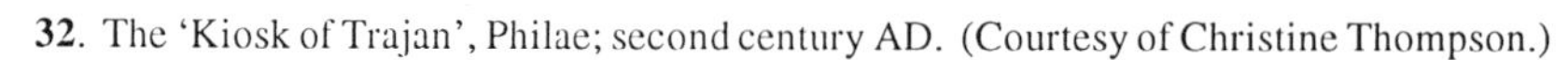

32. The 'Kiosk of Trajan', Philae; second century AD. (Courtesy of Christine Thompson.)

33. Wall painting of Harpocrates and a sphinx, from granary C65 (figure 8) at Karanis; late Roman period. (Author.)

Egyptian Christianity

Many Egyptians had become Christian by the second century AD. The most important Egyptian contribution to the development of Christianity was the invention of monasticism. St Antony was the first to become a hermit and lead an ascetic life in the desert. He died in AD 356 aged 105. Many Egyptians followed his example. They formed a loose community of over 1600 buildings strung out over the desert south-west of the Nile delta, which was known in ancient times as the Kellia (the Cells). Surveys by French archaeologists have recorded many colourful paintings on the walls of their rooms, showing the figures of saints, flowers and animals. They also seem to have enjoyed a wide range of exotic wines and olive oils (figure 26), which were hardly commensurate with an ascetic life.

In AD 315 St Pachomius gathered some monks together in the same building and formed the first monastery, near Thebes. Some monasteries built in the fourth to fifth centuries AD still operate today under the aegis of the Coptic church, such as the Red and White monasteries.

Most of the pagan temples continued to operate until at least the late fourth century AD, but by the sixth century AD they would all have been abandoned. Many were turned into small villages (figure 14) or were converted into churches.

The head of the Egyptian church was the patriarch in Alexandria. The Egyptian church had a long history of theological disputes with the established churches at Rome and Constantinople. The final split came over a doctrinal problem in AD 451. After this time the authority of the church of Rome and Constantinople was purely nominal.

Life and death

The most dangerous time of life in the ancient world was childhood. For Egyptians disease was not the only problem:

> 'If by chance you have a baby, if it is a boy keep it, if it is a girl, dispose of it. You said through Aphrodisias "Don't forget me." How can I forget you? Please don't worry.' (POxy 744 1 BC.)

34. Hermione 'Grammatike', the teacher. One of the earliest known mummy portraits. Hawara; first century AD. (The Mistress and Fellows, Girton College, Cambridge.)

When childhood was past, half of each generation could still expect to die every fifteen years. Medicine for the most part consisted of herbal remedies or magical charms confided to small scraps of papyrus or amulets. Brother-sister marriages and large families were the Egyptian ways of ensuring that at least part of the family name and property survived. Beautiful panel portraits placed above the faces of Roman mummies attest to the failure of many such dreams.

Mummification of a sort continued to be practised throughout the classical period to secure a successful afterlife. Plaster face masks like the more elaborate Pharaonic examples were replaced by a painted portrait of the deceased in Roman times (figure 34). These were painted in hot wax on canvas or wood that was sometimes covered with a thin layer of plaster. The technique was known in ancient times as 'encaustic' painting. The painter needed to work quickly before the wax solidified, but the hot climate helped. The face may have been completed by modelling the semi-solidified wax when it was already on the canvas.

Burial practices continued much as in Pharaonic times. The poor would be given little more than a hole in the sand, but the rich Alexandrian aristocrats had large vaulted chambers with statues and wall paintings in a mixture of classical and Egyptian traditions.

7
Egypt in the classical world

Egypt was always an uncomfortable member of the classical world. In Ptolemaic times native Egyptian resentment against Greeks often made itself felt in personal attacks and riots. Unfortunately our documents tell of such matters only in an oblique way. As time went on Greeks and Egyptians intermarried but cultural and ethnic differences remained. The kings were generous in their treatment of the traditional Egyptian temples and yet few Greeks actively participated in Egyptian cults.

Some modern historians claim that Egypt was never fully part of the Roman Empire, while others would point to classical influence on culture, literature and civic government. Alan Bowman (1986) concludes that classical culture and Egyptian culture were 'layered'. He means by this that the two cultures often existed side by side. There was a native Egyptian literature and a Greek literature; there were classical gods and native Egyptian gods. Some people such as aristocrats and peasants were stuck in one particular culture, whilst others were able to live within both cultures on different levels.

The most popular image of Egypt in the art of the Roman period was the 'Nilotic' mosaic, which could be found on the floors of houses all over the Empire, most famously at Palestrina in Italy. The conception is of a watery landscape, surrounded by reed huts and exotic animals such as crocodiles and hippopotami. Several Egyptian obelisks were removed from the country in the Roman period and set up in the circuses that were used for chariot racing, first at Rome and later across the Empire. The first obelisk was imported by Augustus from the solar sanctuary of Heliopolis. The Romans knew that the obelisk represented the sun and they saw the chariots circling it as the planets. For most Romans Egypt was a symbol of the exotic (figure 37), just as the Orient was for nineteenth-century Europeans, who also imported obelisks, such as the one known as Cleopatra's Needle, now on the Embankment in London.

Some Egyptian habits were alien to classical culture. Brother-sister marriages were an accepted part of Egyptian society from the king downwards but were prohibited in Roman law as incest. Roman law gave strong protection to the rights of the property owner. Egyptian law, at least as represented in the house-sale papyri, emphasises the provision of shared rights. It would be wrong to conclude from this that Egyptian culture was more libertarian than classical culture. Egyptian culture was rather able to maintain major elements of the pre-classical Semitic civilisations that had been subjected to classical influence un-

35. (Left) Stone relief, presumably a tomb, from Oxyrhynchus. The man holds some ears of corn and a bunch of grapes, indicating that he is a devotee of Isis. Late Roman period. (Birmingham City Museum, 215.72.)

36. (Below) The tomb of the priest Petosiris, Hermopolis Magna; fourth century BC. The reliefs inside this tomb are famous for the mix of Greek and Egyptian styles of art. (Courtesy of John Ruffle.)

37. Egyptian influence in Italy. The Emperor Hadrian built this artificial river Nile, the Canopus, at his villa at Tivoli, to remind him of his visit to Egypt. Second century AD. (Author.)

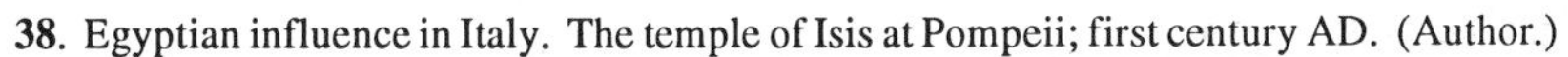

38. Egyptian influence in Italy. The temple of Isis at Pompeii; first century AD. (Author.)

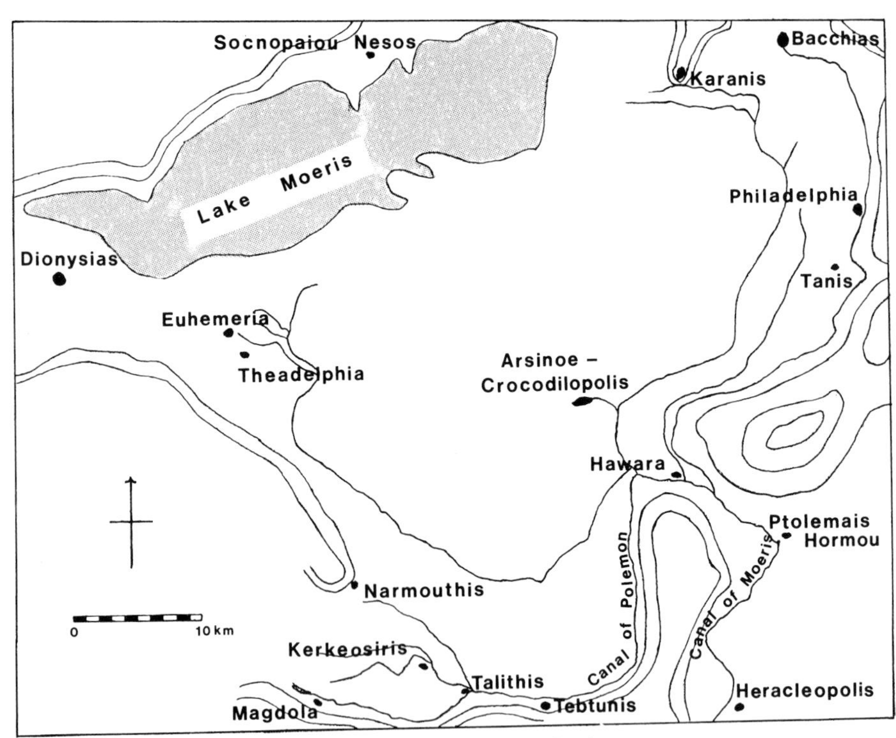

39. Map of known villages in the Fayum region. (Author.)

der Alexander and the Hellenistic monarchies which succeeded him. The continuity of pre-classical traditions in Egypt also reveals something about the Romans, who suppressed such Semitic culture when threatened by it at Carthage but tolerated it in Egypt even when it conflicted with their own law and morals. It was expedient for the Romans to adopt a toleration that made it easier for them to rule the country. Classical culture also viewed Egypt with a grudging respect, as a mysterious civilisation much older than its own (figure 38).

One strange artistic development during late Roman times was the style known as 'Coptic art', which has been seen as an indication of Egyptian independence at the time when the Roman Empire was beginning to fall apart. It is characterised by a retreat from natural depictions and by strange bulging almond-eyed figures. The themes used in stonework, textiles and woodwork were both pagan and Christian. Undoubtedly there were certain features of Egyptian art that were idiosyncratic, but Coptic art falls into a general pattern of the loss of naturalism throughout the Roman world in the third to fourth centuries AD. This style of art survived the Arab conquest of the early seventh century AD and reminds us that even in medieval times Egypt remained a rich country with a strongly independent culture.

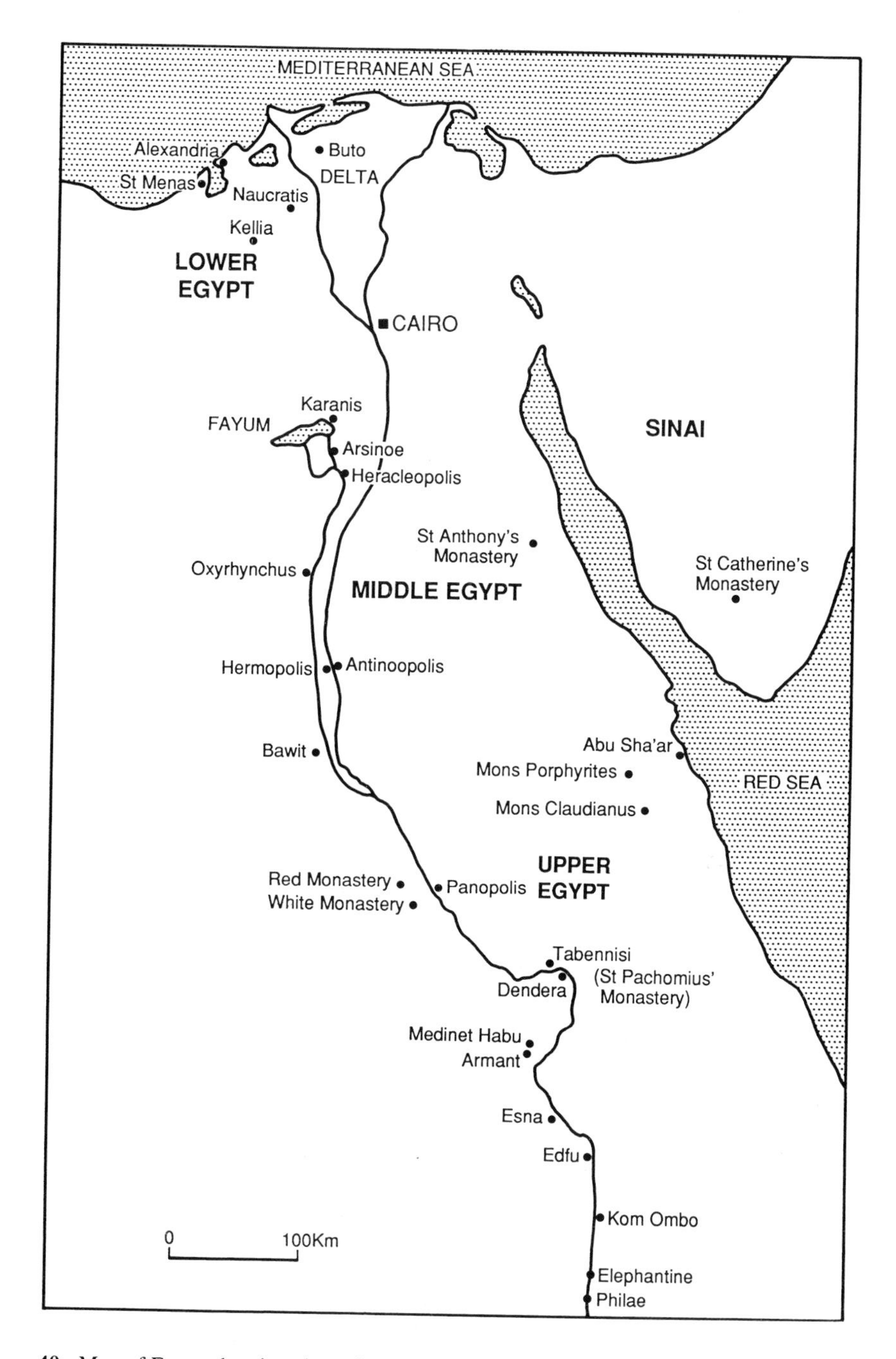

40. Map of Egypt showing sites of the Graeco-Roman Period. (Robert Dizon.)

8
Further reading

General books

Bagnall, R. S. 'Papyrology and Ptolemaic History 1956-80', *Classical World*, 76 (1982-3), 13-21.

Bowman, Alan. *Egypt after the Pharaohs.* British Museum, London, 1986.

Fraser, P. M. *Ptolemaic Alexandria.* Oxford University Press, 1972.

Lewis, Naphtali. *Life in Egypt under Roman Rule.* Oxford University Press, 1983.

Lewis, Naphtali. *Greeks in Ptolemaic Egypt.* Oxford University Press, 1986.

Witt, R. E. *Isis in the Graeco-Roman World.* Thames and Hudson, London, 1971.

Papyrology

Crawford, D. *Kerkeosiris: An Egyptian Village in the Ptolemaic Period.* Cambridge University Press, 1971.

Hunt, A. S., and Edgar, C. C. *Select Papyri* (four volumes). Loeb Classical Library, Harvard, 1932-4.

Montevecchi, O. *La Papirologia.* Società Editrice Internazionale, Turin, 1973.

Taubenschlag, Raphael. *The Law of Greco-Roman Egypt in the Light of the Papyri 332 BC-640 AD.* Herald Square, New York, 1944.

Turner, E. G. *Greek Papyri: An Introduction.* Oxford University Press, second edition 1980.

Zeitschrift für Papyrologie und Epigraphik, 1 (1963) onwards.

Archaeology

Charlesworth, D. 'The Tell El-Fara in Excavation 1969', *Journal of Egyptian Archaeology*, 56 (1970), 19-28.

Du Bourget, P. M. *Coptic Art.* Methuen, London, 1971.

Egloff, M. *Kellia: La Poterie Copte.* Georg, Geneva, 1977.

Giammarusti, A., and Roccati, A. *File: Storia e Vita di un Santuario Egizio.* Ministero degli Affari Esteri, Rome, 1980.

Grenfell, B. P.; Hunt, A. S.; and Hogarth, D. G. *Fayum Towns and their Papyri.* Egypt Exploration Society, London, 1900.

Grossmann, P. *Elephantine II: Kirche und spätantike Hausanlagen im Chnumttempfelhof.* Von Zabern, Mainz, 1980.

Harden, D. *Roman Glass from Karanis.* University of Michigan, Ann Arbor, 1936.

Holscher, U. *The Excavations of Medinet Habu V: The Post-Ramessid Remains.* The Oriental Institute, Chicago, 1954.

Husselman, Elinor M. *Karanis Excavations of the University of Michigan in Egypt 1928-1935: Topography and Architecture.* University of Michigan, Ann Arbor, 1979.

Mond, Sir R., and Myers, O. *Temples of Armant.* Egypt Exploration Society, London, 1940.

Petrie, W. Flinders. *Ehnasya 1904.* Egypt Exploration Society, London, 1905.

Rodziewicz, M. *Alexandrie III: Les habitations romaines tardives d'Alexandrie.* Centre d'Archéologie Méditerranéenne. Warsaw, 1984.

Volbach, W. F. *Il Tessuto nell'Arte Antica.* Fratelli Fabbri, Milan, 1966.

Walters, C. C. *Monastic Archaeology in Egypt.* Aris and Phillips, Warminster, 1974.

Zitterkopf, R. E., and Sidebotham, S. E. 'Stations and Towns on the Quseir-Nile Road', *Journal of Egyptian Archaeology*, 75 (1989), 155-90.

Collections of papyri cited in text

BGU *Ägyptische Urkunden aus den Museen zu Berlin*, nine volumes. Berlin, 1895-1937.

PGiss *Griechische Papyri in Museen des Oberfessischen Geschichtsvereins zu Giessen*, three volumes. Leipzig, 1910-12.

PHib *The Hibeh Papyri*, two volumes. London, 1906 and 1956.

PLond *Greek Papyri in the British Museum*, five volumes. London, 1893-1917.

PMich *Michigan Papyri.* Ann Arbor, 1931 to present.

PMon *Veröffentlichungen aus der Papyrus Sammlung der K. Hof und Staatsbibliothek zu München.* Leipzig, 1914.

POsl *Papyri Osloensis*, three volumes. Oslo, 1925-36.

POxy *Oxyrhynchus Papyri.* Oxford, 1896 to present.

PPetr *The Flinders Petrie Papri*, three volumes. Dublin, 1891-1905.

PRyl *Catalogue of the Greek Papyri in the John Rylands Library*, four volumes. Manchester, 1911-65.

PSI *Pubblicazione della Societa Italiana per la ricerca dei papiri greci e latini in Egitto.* Florence, 1911 to present.

PSt Pal *Studien zur Paläographie und Papyruskunde*, 23 volumes. Leipzig, 1904-22.

PTebt *The Tebtunis Papyri*, five volumes. London, 1902-76.

SB *Sammelbuch Griechischer Urkunden aus Ägypten.* Strasbourg, 1913 to present.

9
Museums

In most cases museums that contain Egyptian objects will have a small area set aside for the Graeco-Roman period. Intending visitors are advised to find out opening times before making a special journey, and to check that relevant items are on display.

United Kingdom

Ashmolean Museum of Art and Archaeology, Beaumont Street, Oxford OX1 2PH. Telephone: 0865 278000. Home of the Oxyrhynchus collection.

Birmingham Museum and Art Gallery, Chamberlain Square, Birmingham, West Midlands B3 3DH. Telephone: 021-235 2834.

Bolton Museum and Art Gallery, Le Mans Crescent, Bolton, Lancashire BL1 1SE. Telephone: 0204 22311 extension 2191.

The British Museum, Great Russell Street, London WC1B 3DG. Telephone: 071-636 1555. Substantial numbers of objects on display, and a large collection of papyri.

City of Bristol Museum and Art Gallery, Queen's Road, Bristol, Avon BS8 1RL. Telephone: 0272 273571.

Durham University Oriental Museum, Elvet Hill, Durham DH1 3TH. Telephone: 091-374 2911.

Fitzwilliam Museum, Trumpington Street, Cambridge CB2 1RB. Telephone: 0223 332900.

Liverpool Museum, William Brown Street, Liverpool, Merseyside L8 8EN. Telephone: 051-207 0001.

The Manchester Museum, The University of Manchester, Oxford Road, Manchester M13 9PL. Telephone: 061-275 2634.

Museum of the School of Archaeology and Oriental Studies, University of Liverpool, PO Box 147, Liverpool L69 3BX. Telephone: 051-709 6022 extension 3086.

The Petrie Museum of Egyptian Archaeology, University College, Gower Street, London WC1E 6BT. Telephone: 071-387 7050 extension 2884.

Royal Museum of Scotland, Chambers Street, Edinburgh EH1 1JF. Telephone: 031-225 7534.

Victoria and Albert Museum, Cromwell Road, South Kensington, London SW7 2RL. Telephone: 071-938 8500.

Whitworth Art Gallery, The University of Manchester, Oxford Road, Manchester M15 6ER. Telephone: 061-273 4865. An important collection of papyri is also kept at the John Rylands Library.

Belgium

Musées Royaux d'Art et d'Histoire, Avenue J. F. Kennedy, 1040, Brussels.

Canada

Royal Ontario Museum, 100 Queen's Park, Toronto, Ontario M5C 2C6.

Egypt

Coptic Museum, St George Street, Old Cairo.
The Egyptian National Museum, Midan el-Tahir, Kasr el-Nil, Cairo.
Greco-Roman Museum, Museum Street 5, Alexandria.

France

Musée du Louvre, Palais du Louvre, F-75041 Paris.

Germany

Ägyptisches Museum, Schloßstrasse 70, 1000 Berlin 19.
Ägyptisches Museum, Staatliche Museen, Bodestrasse 1-3, 102 Berlin.

Italy

Museo Archeologico, Via della Colonna 36, Florence.
Museo Egizio, Musei Vaticani, Viale Vaticano, Rome.
Museo Egizio, Palazzo dell'Accademia delle Scienze, Via Accademia delle Scienze 6, Turin.

United States of America

Brooklyn Museum, 200 Eastern Parkway, Brooklyn, New York 11238.
Cleveland Museum of Art, 11150 East Boulevard, Cleveland, Ohio 44106.
Dumbarton Oaks Research Library and Collection, 1703 32nd Street, NW, Washington DC 20007.
Kelsey Museum of Ancient and Medieval Archaeology, University of Michigan, 434 South State Street, Ann Arbor, Michigan 48109. Contains finds from excavations at Karanis, including large numbers of papyri.
Metropolitan Museum of Art, 5th Avenue at 82nd Street, New York, NY 10028.
Museum of Fine Arts, 465 Huntington Avenue, Boston, Massachusetts 02115.
The Textile Museum, 2320 South Street, NW, Washington DC 20008.
University of Chicago Oriental Institute Museum, 1155 East 58th Street, Chicago, Illinois 60637.

Index

Page numbers in italic refer to illustrations.